## TO THE EXTREME

# BMX Freestyle

### By Matt Doeden

Reading Consultant:
Barbara J. Fox
Reading Specialist
North Carolina State University

Capstone
press

Mankato, Minnesota

Blazers is published by Capstone Press,
151 Good Counsel Drive, P.O. Box 669, Mankato, Minnesota 56002.
www.capstonepress.com

*Library of Congress Cataloging-in-Publication Data*
Doeden, Matt.
  BMX freestyle / by Matt Doeden.
    p. cm.—(Blazers. To the extreme)
  Includes bibliographical references and index.
  ISBN-13: 978-0-7368-2728-7 (hardcover)
  ISBN-10: 0-7368-2728-5 (hardcover)
  ISBN-13: 978-0-7368-5224-1 (softcover pbk.)
  ISBN-10: 0-7368-5224-7 (softcover pbk.)
    1. Bicycle motocross—Juvenile literature. [1. Bicycle motocross.
2. Extreme sports.] I. Title. II. Series: Doeden, Matt. Blazers. To the
extreme.
GV1049.3.D64 2005
796.9'6—dc22                                        2003026625

Summary: Describes the sport of BMX freestyle, including tricks and
  safety information.

**Editorial Credits**
Angela Kaelberer, editor; Jason Knudson, designer; Jo Miller,
  photo researcher; Eric Kudalis, product planning editor


**Photo Credits**
Corbis/Duomo, 13; NewSport/Al Fuchs, cover
David A. Dobbs, 27
Getty Images/Elsa, 23; Ezra Shaw, 20; Stanley Chou, 12, 19, 21;
  T-Mobile/Mark Mainz, 5, 6, 7, 8, 17
SportsChrome Inc./Rob Tringali Jr., 28–29
TransWorld BMX/Keith Mulligan, 11, 14–15, 18, 25

1  2  3  4  5  6  09  08  07  06  05  04

# Table of Contents

# Motocross for Bikes

A BMX rider drops into a halfpipe ramp. He comes up the other side and sails into the air.

Coping

Halfpipe ramp

The rider lands and grinds his
bike along the coping. He does a
no-hander off the ramp.

The rider grabs the handlebars. He twists the bike until it is almost flat in the air. He will do more tricks before he finishes his run.

## BLAZER FACT

Kids doing motocross moves on their bicycles started the sport of BMX.

# BMX Bikes

Freestyle bikes have small wheels and wide tires. The wide tires help riders balance during tricks.

Many riders add pegs to their
bikes. They stand on the pegs
during tricks.

Peg

# BMX Park Diagram

Roll-in

Transition

Coping

Railing

WOODWARD

Flat-bottom

# Tricks

Vert riders do tricks off ramps. They get big air as their bikes spin and flip.

## BLAZER FACT

Flatland riders don't always have to wear helmets at competitions.

Flatland riders do tricks on level ground. They balance on one wheel. They spin the handlebars.

Street riders do tricks in
skateboard parks and BMX parks.
Riders grind on railings and stairs.
They launch into the air off ramps.

Dirt riders do tricks on dirt courses. They jump over mounds of dirt called doubles.

## BLAZER FACT

When a rider takes both hands and feet off the bike, the trick is called a nothing.

# safety

Crashes can happen to anyone. Helmets protect riders' heads. Visors protect their faces. Riders wear elbow pads and gloves.

Safe riders practice their tricks in BMX parks. These riders look out for each other as they do tricks.

## BLAZER FACT

Both BMX riders and skateboarders use many of the same parks.

# Going for the gold medal!

# Glossary

**flatland** (FLAT-land)—a type of BMX riding involving tricks done on level ground

**freestyle** (FREE-stile)—a type of BMX riding that focuses on tricks, stunts, and jumps

**grind** (GRINDE)—a trick performed by sliding the pegs of a bike across an object

**halfpipe** (HAF-pipe)—a U-shaped ramp with high walls

**motocross** (MOH-toh-kross)—a sport in which people race motorcycles on dirt tracks

**vert** (VURT)—a style of BMX riding done on large ramps called halfpipes

**visor** (VYE-zur)—a clear shield on the front of a helmet

# Read More

**Blomquist, Christopher.** *BMX in the X Games.*
A Kid's Guide to the X Games. New York: PowerKids
Press, 2003.

**Maurer, Tracy.** *BMX Freestyle.* Radsports Guides.
Vero Beach, Fla.: Rourke, 2002.

**Parr, Danny.** *Extreme Bicycle Stunt Riding Moves.*
Behind the Moves. Mankato, Minn.: Capstone
Press, 2001.

# Internet Sites

FactHound offers a safe, fun way to
find Internet sites related to this
book. All of the sites on FactHound
have been researched by our staff.

Here's how:

1. Visit *www.facthound.com*
2. Type in this special code **0736827285**
   for age-appropriate sites. Or enter a
   search word related to this book for a
   more general search.
3. Click on the **Fetch It** button.

FactHound will fetch the best sites for you!

# Index